Test Your Own IQ

Philip Carter and Ken Russell

BARNES
&NOBLE
BOOKS
NEW YORK

ISBN 0-7607-2834-8 (paperback)
ISBN 0-7607-2835-6 (hardcover)

Book design by Lundquist Design, New York

Printed and bound in the United States of America

02 03 04 05 MP 9 8 7 6 5 4 3 2 1
02 03 04 05 HC 9 8 7 6 5 4 3 2 1

Test Your Own IQ

Introduction

Intelligence is the capacity to learn or understand. Every person possesses a single general ability of mind, and it is this ability of mind that determines how efficiently we deal with concrete situations and profit intellectually from sensory experience. This general ability varies in amount from person to person, but remains approximately the same throughout life for any individual.

In psychology, intelligence is thus defined as the capacity to acquire knowledge or understanding, and to use it in novel situations.

What is IQ?

IQ is the abbreviation for intelligence quotient.

Intelligence quotient (IQ) is an age-related measure of intelligence and is defined as 100 times mental age. The word quotient means the result of dividing one quantity by another, and intelligence can be defined as mental ability and quickness of mind.

It is generally agreed that an individual's IQ rating is mainly hereditary and remains constant in development to about the age of thirteen, after which it is shown to slow down; beyond the age of eighteen little or no improvement is found. It is further agreed that the most marked increase in a person's IQ takes place in early childhood. Theories have been put forward recently about different contributory factors—for example, recent experiments in Scandinavia have suggested that increased breast feeding in babies has resulted in a higher IQ, and research in Japan has shown that the playing of computer games by children, which involve a high degree of skill and agility of mind, have also resulted in higher IQ measurement.

What is an IQ test?

An intelligence test (IQ test) is, by definition, any test that purports to measure intelligence. Generally such tests consist of a graded series of tasks, each of which has been standardized with a large representative population of individuals. Such procedure establishes the average IQ as 100.

IQ tests are part of what is generally referred to as psychological testing. Such test content may be addressed to almost any aspect of our intellectual or emotional make-up, including personality, attitude, intelligence, or emotion. In the U.S., as elsewhere, a wide range of such tests are in use. These include achievement tests, which are designed to assess performance in an academic area; aptitude tests, which predict future performance in an area in which the individual is not already trained; objective personality tests, which are designed to provide an overall profile of the personality of the individual being assessed; and intelligence (IQ) tests.

History of testing

The earliest known attempts to rank people in terms of intelligence date back to the Chinese Mandarin system, c. 500 B.C., when studying the works of Confucius enabled successful candidates to enter the public service. The top one percent of candidates were successful in progressing to the next stage, where they would again be run off against each other, and the procedure repeated yet again through a final layer of selection. Thus, the chosen candidates were in the top one percent of the top one percent of the top one percent.

The first modern intelligence test was devised in 1905 by the French psychologists Alfred Binet and Theodore Simon. The pair developed a 30-item test with the purpose of ensuring that no child be denied admittance to the Paris school system without formal examination.

In 1916 the American psychologist Lewis Terman revised the Binet-Simon scale to provide comparison standards for Americans from age three to adulthood. Born in 1877 in Johnson County, Indiana, Terman devised the term intelligence quotient and developed the so-called Stanford-Binet intelligence test to measure IQ after joining the faculty of Stanford University as professor of education. The Stanford-Binet test was further revised in 1937 and 1960 and remains today one of the most widely used of all intelligence tests.

During the 1930s controversies surrounding the definition and make-up of intelligence led to the development of the Wechsler-Bellevue scale of intelligence which as well as measuring general mental ability, also revealed patterns of intellectual strengths and weaknesses. The Wechsler tests extend from pre-school to adult age range and are now as prominent as the Stanford-Binet test.

How exactly is IQ measured?

When measuring the IQ of a child, the subject will take an IQ test that has been standardized with an average score recorded for each age group. Thus a child of ten years of age who scored the results expected of a child of twelve would have an IQ of 120, calculated as follows:

$$\frac{\text{mental age (12)}}{\text{chronological age (10)}} \quad \text{x} \quad 100 = 120 \text{ IQ}$$

However, because in adulthood little or no improvement in IQ rating is found, adults have to be judged on an IQ test whose average score is 100 and their results graded above and below this norm according to known scores. A properly validated test would have to be given to some 20,000 people and the results correlated before it would reveal an accurate measurement of a person's IQ.

Like most distributions found in nature, the distribution of IQ takes the form of a fairly regular bell curve. On the

Stanford-Binet scale, half the population fall between 90 and 110 IQ, half of them above 100 and half of them below; 25 percent score above 110; 11 percent above 120; 3 percent above 130, and 0.6 percent above 140. At the other end of the scale the same kind of proportion occurs.

Is it possible to improve your IQ?

It is accepted that IQ is hereditary and remains constant throughout life, and therefore, it is not possible to improve your actual IQ.

Paradoxically, it is, however, possible to improve your performance on IQ tests by practicing the many different types of questions, and learning to recognize the recurring themes.

IQ tests are set on the assumption that those taking the test have no knowledge of the scoring method itself, and that they know very little about the question methods within these tests and the required thought process needed to solve them. Logically, therefore, it follows that if you learn something about this form of testing and know how to approach the different kinds of question, you can improve your performance on the actual tests.

Practice on the type of questions included in this book has the advantage of exercising the brain. It is certainly the case that many of us do not exercise our brain sufficiently, yet it is perhaps the most important part of the human body. Apart from being the control center for all our movement, sleep, hunger, and thirst—in fact virtually every activity necessary for survival—it at the same time absorbs and learns from a continual intake of thoughts, feelings, and memories. Additionally, all our emotions, such as aggression, love, hate, elation, and fear, are controlled by the brain. Yet, for many of us the brain is the part of our body that we tend to neglect the most.

What type of questions are you likely to find in an IQ test?

Some IQ tests are constructed quite differently from others. The Stanford-Binet is heavily weighted with items including verbal abilities, while the Wechsler scales consist of two separate verbal and performance subscales, each with its own IQ. The Cattell test, used mainly in the U.K., also has separate tests of verbal and spatial abilities, with separate IQ ratings.

It is said that to have a mastery of words is to have the ability to produce order out of chaos and that command of vocabulary is, thus, a true measure of intelligence. Because of this, vocabulary tests are widely used in intelligence testing.

It is also argued, however, that verbal tests can be biased. They involve prior knowledge of language and word meanings and, because of this, some IQ tests rely on diagrammatic representation rather than verbal abilities. Such questions are regarded as purely exercises of the mind, designed to test raw intelligence, free from the influence of prior knowledge. To solve them you have to apply your mind to each set of diagrams, quickly comprehend the experience before you, and decide what logical patterns and/or sequences are occurring.

In order to give you the opportunity to practice all types of questions you are likely to encounter in actual IQ tests, each of the tests that have been specially compiled for this book contains a mixture of verbal, numerical, and diagrammatic questions, as well as additional questions involving logical thought processes and a degree of lateral thinking.

The following are examples of some of the types of questions you are likely to encounter as you work your way through the tests in this book, as well as a number of warm-up questions for you to attempt. We recommend that you work your way through all these sample and warm-up questions before moving to the actual tests.

Classification

A classification test is, generally, any test in which the subject is required to sort the materials into classes. In this book we present these tests as questions where you are required to find the odd one out in a group of words, numbers, or diagrams. In order to solve such questions you must consider what all the other items have in common. For example, before deciding which one of a group of five diagrams is the odd one out you must decide what feature or condition is possessed by four of these diagrams that is not shared by the fifth diagram.

Examples:
Which is the odd one out?

i) Verbal

elevate, increase, raise, lift, hoist

Answer: Increase. The rest are words meaning to move upwards. Increase means to grow or expand.

ii) Diagrammatical

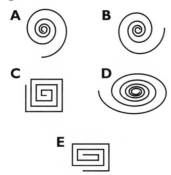

Answer: B. It spirals counterclockwise from the center; the rest spiral clockwise from the center.

iii) Numerical

342, 798, 243, 196, 897

Answer: 196. The others are in reverse pairs, i.e. 342/243, 798/897.

Warm-up Classification Test

In each of the following, which is the odd one out?

1. disciple, pupil, student, tutor, scholar

2. 729, 347, 618, 426, 549

3.

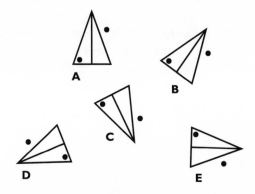

4. 482, 761, 536, 293, 647

5. laugh, joke, smirk, giggle, titter

Answers:

1. Tutor. A tutor is a teacher, the rest are learners.

2. 618. In all the others the first two digits are equal to the third digit when added together: $7 + 2 = 9$.

3. C. The rest are the same figure rotated; C is a mirror image of the rest.

4. 647. Its digits total 17, whereas the digits of the other numbers total 14.

5. Joke. The rest are expressions of mirth or amusement. A joke is something that may, or may not, invoke such reactions.

Synonyms

A synonym is a word having a similar meaning as another in the same language. For example, synonyms of the word correct are in one sense: accurate, exact, flawless, faultless; in another sense: amend, rectify, remedy; and in yet another sense: admonish, discipline, chastise.

Example:

i) Which word in the brackets is closest in meaning to the word in capitals?

ERR (change, miscalculate, shift, remove, espouse)

Answer: Miscalculate is closest in meaning to the word err.

ii) Which two words are closest in meaning?

underrate, misquote, transgress, distort, mistrust, blend

Answer: Misquote and distort are the two words closest in meaning.

Warm-up Synonym Test

1. Which word in the brackets is closest in meaning to the word in capitals?

QUICK (latent, total, swift, anxious, ready)

2. Which two words are closest in meaning?

happiness, hope, amity, desire, humor, grace

3. Complete the circles with two words, one in each circle reading clockwise, that are similar in meaning. You have to find the starting points, and provide the missing letters.

4. Which two words are closest in meaning?

clutch, beat, cosset, embrace, relate, boast

5. Which word in the brackets is closest in meaning to the word in capitals?

DISCERNIBLE (fundamental, visible, opaque, shrewd, believable)

Answers:

1. swift

2. hope, desire

3. gigantic, colossal

4. clutch, embrace

5. visible

Antonyms

An antonym is a word meaning the opposite of another word in the same language. For example, the word left is the opposite to the word right, and the word graceful is the opposite of the word clumsy.

Example:

i) Which word in brackets is the most opposite in meaning of the word in capitals?

FRESH (raw, late, asleep, weary, rest)

Answer: The word raw is the opposite of the word fresh,

ii) Which two words are most opposite in meaning?

buy, barter, estimate, sell, find, trade

Answer: The words buy and sell are the most opposite in meaning.

Warm-up Antonym Test

1. Which two words are most opposite in meaning?

enlarge, contradict, last, agree, provide, convene

2. Complete the circles with two words, one in each circle reading clockwise, that are opposite in meaning. You have to find the starting points, and provide the missing letters.

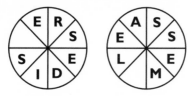

3. Which word in brackets is most opposite in meaning to the word in capitals?

HUMANE (arrogant, sultry, brutal, sad, petulant)

4. Which two words are most opposite in meaning?

modest, quiet, polite, radical, insulting, awkward

5. Which two words are most opposite in meaning?

liberate, appease, appraise, disappear, enrage, hoodwink

Answers:

1. contradict, agree

2. disperse, assemble

3. brutal

4. polite, insulting

5. appease, enrage

Analogy

An analogy is a relationship between two things where it is necessary to reason the answer from a parallel relationship.

In an analogy test a relationship between two terms is given and the test taker is required to complete an analogous relationship. Questions typically take the form: A is to B as C is to ?; alternatively, they may be presented as A : B C : ?

Examples:

i) Verbal:

casino : gambling

mosque : a. church
          b. worship
          c. Muslim
          d. dome
          e. God

The correct answer is b. worship, the analogy is that worship takes place in a mosque and gambling takes place in a casino.

ii) Numerical:

   64 : 24

   29 : a. 14
        b. 16
        c. 17
        d. 18
        e. 20

The correct answer is d. 18 because 6 x 4 = 24 and 2 x 9 = 18.

iii) Diagrammatical:

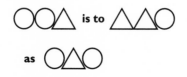

The correct answer is A. Circles change to triangles and vice versa.

1. foreword : book

       overture: a. play
                  b. composer
                  c. orchestra
                  d. opera
                  e. music

2. 6381 : 3618

    5912 : a. 2195
            b. 1528
            c. 9152
            d. 1925
            e. 9521

3.

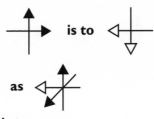

is to

as

is to:

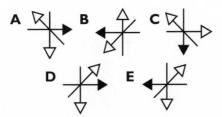

4. resign : politician

       abdicate : a. throne
                b. prince
                c. monarch
                d. empire
                e. retire

5.

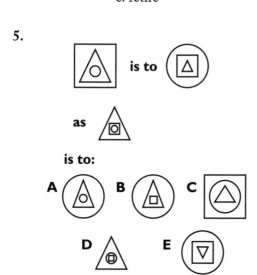

Answers:

1. d. Opera. An overture precedes an opera as a foreword precedes a book.

2. e. 9521. The first two numbers reverse, and so do the last two numbers.

3. D. The arrowheads move from one end of the arm to the other and change from black to white and vice versa.

4. c. Monarch. A politician resigns from office and a monarch abdicates from the throne.

5. B. The figure originally in the center goes to the outside, the figure originally in the middle goes to the center and the figure originally on the outside goes to the middle.

Anagrams

An anagram is the transposition of the letters of a word or phrase to form a new word or phrase.

The most simple anagrams are where the letters of a word are scrambled and the subject must find what word the letters spell. For example, the letters ganmara can be rearranged to spell the word anagram.

The majority of anagram questions in this book are word anagrams, in which a word

(or words) is given that must be rearranged to find another word or phrase. For example, the letters of the word HORSE can be rearranged to spell the word SHORE.

Examples:

i) NICE BAT is an anagram of what 7-letter word?

Answer: cabinet

ii) NORTH SLOG is an anagram of what two words that are opposite in meaning?

Answer: long, short

Warm-up Anagram Test

1. RUN TO CLAN is an anagram of what 9-letter word?

2. FIRED FOB is an anagram of what two words that are similar in meaning?

3. Which of the following is not an anagram of a boy's name?

    > sbila
    > karnf
    > vaddi
    > srido
    > nhyre

4. MAD LEER is an anagram of which precious stone?

5. JOVE RISEN is an anagram of what two words that are opposite in meaning?

Answers:

1. nocturnal

2. offer, bid

3. srido = Doris. The boy's names are: Basil, Frank, David and Henry

4. emerald

5. join, sever

Calculation and Logic

Besides the examples quoted above, there are many other tests that involve calculation and logic.

Approximately one-third of the tests in this book are number tests of one kind or another, most of them involving number series or simple calculations. Many of these tests involve flexibility of thought and a degree of lateral thinking, and the more you practice these little puzzles, the more proficient you become at solving them.

Examples:

i) What number comes next in this sequence?

1, 3, 7, 15, 31, ?

Answer:

63. The amount being added doubles each time: 1+2=3; 3+4=7; 7+8=15; 15+16=31; 31+32=63.

ii) What number should replace the question mark?

2 4 6

3 1 4

5 5 ?

Answer:

10. The third number in each row and column is the sum of the first two numbers.

Warm-up Calculation and Logic Test

1. Alan has twice as many as Tim. Between them they have 39. How many does each have?

2. What number should replace the question mark?

3. What number continues this sequence?

100, 98, 93, 85, 74, ?

4. What number should replace the question mark?

3	7	4
1	4	2
6	5	9

5	9	3
3	6	1
8	7	?

5. How many minutes is it before 12 noon if one hour ago it was five times as many minutes past 9 a.m.?

Answers:

1. Alan has 26 and Tim has 13.

2. 4. Numbers in opposite segments always add up to 11.

3. 60. The amount subtracted each time increases by 3: 100–2=98; 98–5=93; 93–8=85; 85–11=74; 74–14=60.

4. 8. Looking at numbers in the same position in each grid, the first two columns in the second grid are plus 2, and in the third column they are minus 1.

5. 20 minutes. 11:40 less 1 hour = 10:40. 9 a.m. plus 100 minutes (20 x 5) = 10:40.

All the above examples are designed to give you a flavor of the kind of questions you will encounter in the tests that follow, but it is by no means a complete list. There are several unique question types, and there are other types of verbal, diagrammatical, and numerical questions that regularly occur. You will become familiar with them as you work your way through this book.

How to use this book

The book consists of ten separate tests, each with 40 questions. The tests are of approximately the same degree of difficulty.

All the tests have been specially compiled for this book, so they have not been validated. Therefore, a precise IQ rating cannot be given. Nevertheless, we have given a performance assessment for each test, together with an approximate IQ rating, and the top percentage of population to which this equates. There is also an accumulative rating for all ten tests.

A time limit of ninety minutes is allowed for each test. The correct answers are given at the end of each test, together with detailed explanations. You should award yourself 1 point for each question answered correctly, except in rare cases where a bonus point is indicated. You must keep strictly to the time limit, otherwise your score will be invalid. You should not, therefore, spend too much time on any one question. If you do not know the answer, it is always worth guessing—as intuition is often proved to be correct! You should, however, take time to read the instructions to each question. If, at the end of the test you find you have time to spare, utilize that time to make a quick review of your answers. We have all been guilty of slips of the pen at some time or another, and this may be one of those occasions.

Please note that calculators may be used to assist with solving numerical questions if you prefer.

One test

Score	Rating	Approximate IQ rating	% of the population
36-40	Exceptional	140 or above	top 1%
31-35	Excellent	130–139	top 3%
25-30	Very Good	121–129	top 11%
19-24	Good	111–120	top 25%
12-18	Average	90–110	top 50%

All ten tests

Score	Rating	Approximate IQ rating	% of the population
351-400	Exceptional	140 or above	top 1%
301-350	Excellent	130–139	top 3%
241-300	Very Good	121–129	top 11%
181-240	Good	111–120	top 25%
120-180	Average	90–110	top 50 %

Test One Questions

1.

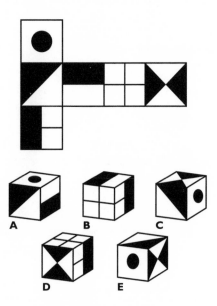

When the above is folded to form a cube, which is the only one of the following that can be produced?

2.   N   A   *

       O   L   C

       *   A   T

Start at a corner letter and spiral round the perimeter clockwise to spell out a nine-letter word, finishing at the center square. You must provide the missing letters.

3. A phrase has had all its vowels removed and has been split into groups of three letters. What is the phrase? All remaining letters are in the same order.

   MTL DMR TNS CTY

4. Which number is the odd one out?

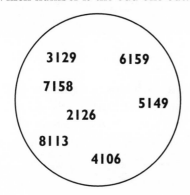

5.

What comes next?

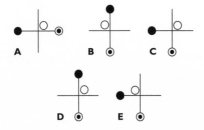

6. What word can be placed on the end of these words to make new words?

> AM
> UP
> ADD
> PORT
> WEEK

7. Insert a pair of letters in each set of parentheses so that they finish the word on the left and start the new word on the right. When inserted, the correct letters will spell out an 8-letter word when read downwards in pairs.

> LI (**) AT
> SA (**) TE
> MO (**) OP
> RE (**) CH

8. A backpacker averages 22 miles a day for 7 days. The number of miles he walks on the eighth day raises his average to 23 miles per day. How many miles would he have had to walk to raise his average to 25 miles per day?

9. Which three of the four pieces below can be fitted together to form a perfect square?

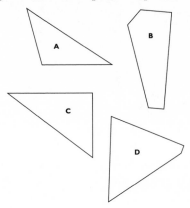

10. Which word in the brackets is closest in meaning to the word in capitals?

PRESCIENT
(decent, psychic, needful, eminent, sandy)

11. Clara has a third again as many as Louisa, and Alice has a third again as many as Clara. Altogether they have 185. How many has each?

12. Fill in the blanks to find four words that are all synonyms of OVERJOYED.

*U*H*R*C
*U*I*A*T
*H*I*L*D
*L*T*D

13. Which is the odd one out?

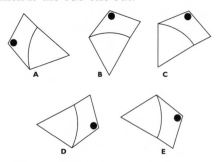

14. Which word in the brackets is most opposite in meaning to the word in capitals?

DENY (forfeit, sadness, denude, confirm, explain)

15. Insert the letters into the diagram to spell out two related words:

```
        *
        *
        *
* * * * T * * *
        *
        *
```

U C L
C G E
R I I
E R A

16. What number should replace the question mark?

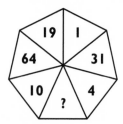

17.

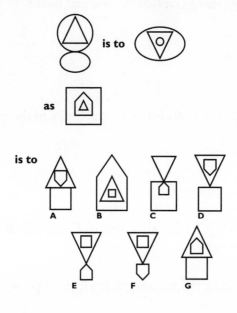

18. hematite : iron

     galena : a) copper
              b) mercury
              c) lead
              d) zinc
              e) tin

19. Solve the anagram in the parentheses to correctly complete the quotation by John Stuart Mill.

     The (TRUE APPLE) obstacle to human advancement is custom.

20. What number should replace the question mark?

    3829 : 517
    7416 : 810
    5348 : ?

21. Which word in brackets is the most opposite to the word in capitals?

    DOCILITY (exhaustion, plausible, doggedness, imperious, firmness, overwhelmed)

22. HEY! GIANT SONG is an anagram of which familiar phrase (8, 4 letters)?

23. Place two 3-letter bits together to produce a type of vehicle.

    DRO HER HAN OPY DEN GER

    SON DOD JAL TAN RSE SKI

24. Produce a 6-letter word out of only these four letters.

    E T

    X S

25. Complete the circles to find two words that are antonyms. The words may appear clockwise or counterclockwise.

26. What 11-letter word is suggested below?

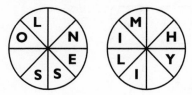

27. Which two words are closest in meaning?

relax, authorize, hinder, tolerate, consider, enervate

28.

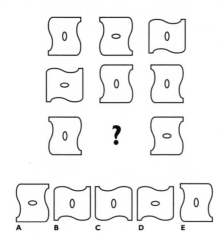

29. Place two 4-letter segments together to produce an 8-letter word that is a type of food.

CHES JACK ROLL FLAP COWS

OMER HAZE LNIT MAPS TNIT

30. Find an 11-letter word or name by tracing from letter to connected letter. Letters are traced across the circle by the chords; however, if the next letter is four letters or less away in the alphabet from the previous letter, it will be found by tracing around the circumference.

31. What is a canticle?

   a. a church spire
   b. mechanical ram
   c. a hymn
   d. priest's cloak

32.

Which comes next?

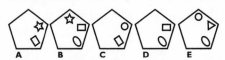

33. What number, if you :

add 8 to it
then add 6 to it
then subtract 7 1/9
then multiply by 9
Equals 324?

34. What number should replace the question mark?

1, 4, 6, 14, 26, 54, ?

35.

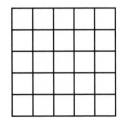

Produce four 4-letter words into the grid, one per line, by using the letters of the phrase DETAIN WANTED AIDE; use each letter only once. The four words when placed correctly in the grid will form a magic word square, where all four words appear both horizontally and vertically.

36. Find an 8-letter word with the aid of the clue *doesn't sound good*, that when placed on the bottom line will complete eight 3-letter words reading downwards.

M	A	T	A	A	T	W	H
A	D	A	C	L	I	A	A
*	*	*	*	*	*	*	*

37. Insert the remaining letters to find the names of two types of bird:

```
        *
        *                    R O P R E V C D L N
      * O * * * *
        *
        *
        *
```

38. What number should replace the question mark?

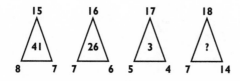

39.

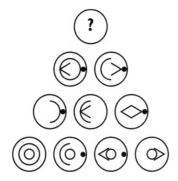

Which circle below should replace the question mark?

40. What number should replace the question mark?

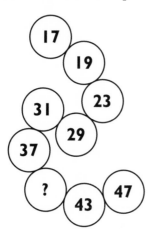

Test One Answers

1. C.

2. Octagonal.

3. Mutual admiration society.

4. 2126. In all the other numbers, the first and last digits added together equal the middle two digits, as in 3129, where 3 + 9 = 12.

5. C. The black circle moves clockwise to an arm in turn, the white circle moves counterclockwise one corner in turn, and the circle with the dot moves backwards and forwards between two arms.

6. End. Produces: amend, upend, addend, portend, and weekend.

7. Megastar.

8. 46 miles: 7 days = 154 (22 miles per day)

   8 days = 184 (30 miles walked)
   8 days = 200 (46 miles walked)

9.

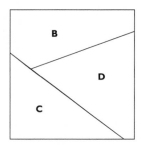

10. Psychic.

11. Alice 80, Clara 60, Louisa 45.

12. Euphoric, jubilant, thrilled, elated.

> Score one point for 2 correct and a bonus point for all 4 correct!

13. D. The rest are all the same figure rotated.

14. Confirm.

15. Electric guitar.

16. 46. Start at 1 and work clockwise to alternate segments adding 3, 6, 9, 12, 15, 18: 1 + 3 = 4, 4 + 6 = 10, etc.

17. A. The analogy of the first two figures are reversed. The square reduces and goes to the bottom, the house end inverts and goes inside the triangle, which increases in size.

18. Lead.

19. Perpetual.

20. 911: 5 + 4 = 9, 3 + 8 = 11

21. Imperious.

22. Anything goes!

23. Jalopy.

24. Sextet.

25. Boldness, humility.

26. Interlinked.

27. Relax, enervate.

28. B. In each line and column the large figures are positioned in three different ways. In each line and column there is one horizontal inner ellipse.

29. Flapjack.

30. Nightingale.

31. C. A hymn.

32. B. At each alternate stage, a new figure is introduced at the top. At the next stage, all figures move down one place and the bottom figure disappears.

33. 29

34. Alternately multiply by 2 and add 2, then multiply by 2 and subtract 2.

35.

W	I	N	D
I	D	E	A
N	E	A	T
D	A	T	E

36. Toneless.

37. Plover, condor.

38. 80: (7 x 14) − 18

39. A. Each pair of circles produce the circle above by carrying forward only those elements that are different. Similar elements are cancelled out.

40. 41. A series of prime numbers from 17 to 47.

Test Two Questions

1. How many lines appear below?

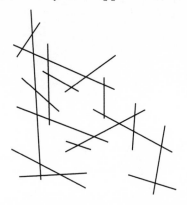

2. Which two words are most opposite in meaning?

potent, complete, overt, coercive, trivial, ulterior

3. Solve the anagram in parentheses to correctly complete the quotation by Mark Twain.

Loyalty to (TEPID FIRE) opinion never yet broke a chain or forced a human soul.

4. What number should replace the question mark?

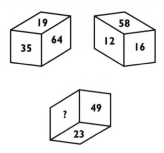

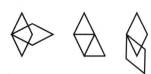

5.

What comes next?

6. Which two words are closest in meaning?

remote, itinerant, nomadic, insulated, guide, saucy

7. Unscramble these three anagrammed words to determine what they have in common.

bulge   argon   stair

8. What number should replace the question mark?

9. Which is the odd one out?

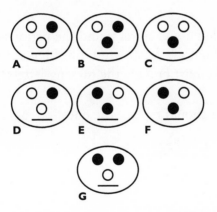

10. Insert the name of a fruit into the bottom line to complete the 3-letter words reading downwards.

A	F	T	P	C	F	F	M	M
R	A	E	A	U	O	I	A	A
*	*	*	*	*	*	*	*	*

11.

D	U	*
N	E	A
E	L	*

Start at a corner letter and spiral round the perimeter clockwise to spell out a 9-letter word, finishing at the center square. You must provide the missing letters.

12. What number should replace the question mark?

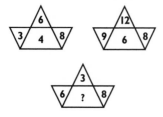

13.

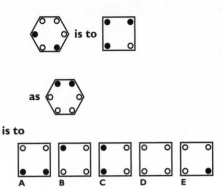

14. clarion : trumpet

        musette :a. flute
                  b. bagpipe
                  c. oboe
                  d. tuba
                  e. trombone

15. Fill in the missing word to complete the crossword

```
    J           F
S U B M A R I N E
    N           E       *
    K           I     Y * C H T
                G       *
  L A U N C H   H       *
                T A N K E R
    C A N O E
                R
```

16. Which number is the odd one out?

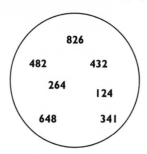

17.

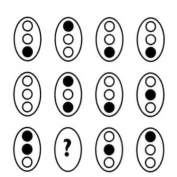

What should replace the question mark?

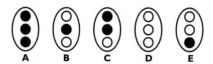

18. SHINY WARE is an anagram of what two words that are similar in meaning?

19. Complete the words so that the two letters that end the first word start the second word and the two letters that end the second word start the third word, etc. The two letters that end the fifth word start the first word, to complete the circle.

* * T A * *

* * A N * *

* * R E * *

* * L U * *

* * P E * *

20. What number should replace the question mark?

246, 458, 8610, 16712, ?

21. Fill in the blanks to complete a word meaning *minute particle*.

* * * P U S C * *

22. Which two words are similar in meaning?

untruthful, scarcity, ephemeral, particular, evanescent, appraisal

23.

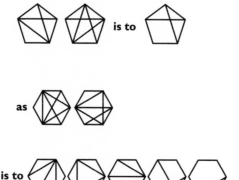

24. Which word in brackets is most opposite in meaning to the word in capitals?

EMBROIL (instigate, castigate, disentangle, propriety, paroxysm)

25. Arrange the two 5-letter words to find two more related 5-letter words made famous in legend.

LEARN DOUBT

26. What number should replace the question mark?

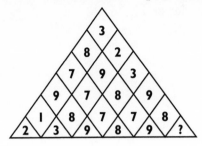

27. Insert a word that finishes the first word and starts the second:

SON   * * *   WORK

28.

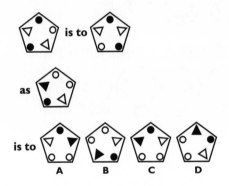

29. Which of the following is not an anagram of a word beginning with the letter T?

> city pal
> hat tree
> fit says
> Mr. Taunt

30.

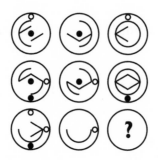

Which circle should replace the question mark?

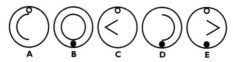

31. What color is cornelian?

> a. dull red
> b. mauve
> c. green
> d. light blue

32. What letter should replace the question mark?

33. SMART ROBIN is an anagram of what 10-letter word?

34. Take one letter from each of these four types of fish in turn to spell out another type of fish.

CUTTLE
BREAM
LOACH
TUNNY
SKATE

35.

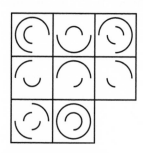

Which is the missing tile?

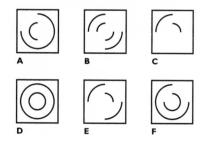

36. Place two 4-letter bits together to produce an 8-letter word that is a type of bird.

DABC LINC GROS THRA GAME COCE
SMET BEAK STAR HICE

37. Complete the circles to find two words that are synonyms. The words may appear clockwise or counterclockwise.

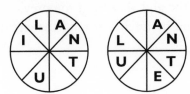

38. What number should replace the question mark?

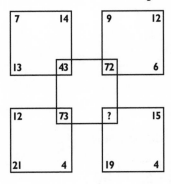

39. Find a 10-letter word or name by tracing from letter to connected letter. Letters are traced across the circle by chords; however, if the next letter is four letters or less away in the alphabet from the previous letter, it will be found by tracing around the circumference.

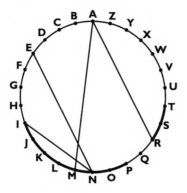

40. Which number is the odd one out?

| 25 | 35 | 48 | 63 | 80 |

Test Two Answers

1 17.

2. Overt, ulterior.

3. Petrified.

4. 24. Three groups of numbers, one per cube on corresponding sides, add up to 100: 35 + 16 + 49 = 100; 19 + 58 +
   23 = 100; 64 + 12 + 24 = 100.

5. C. One diamond remains stationary while the other diamond pivots 450 clockwise at each stage.

6. Itinerant, nomadic.

7. They are all musical instruments : bugle, organ, sitar.

8. 75. Imagine the dot in the center to be a decimal point.
   Then looking at numbers opposite and working clockwise, add 0.75 each time a sequence appears: 1.5, 2.25,
   3.0, 4.75.

9. B. A is the same as E with black/white reversal; similarly
   C is the same as G, and D is the same as F.

10. Cranberry.

11. Endurable.

12. 16: 6 x 8 = 48. 48/3 = 16

13. A. Take out the dots on the extreme right and left in the hexagon, and then change the remaining dots from black to white and vice versa.

14. Bagpipe.

15. Barge.

16. 264. The rest of the numbers are in pairs, ABC/DEF, where D is half of C, F is half of B, and E is half of A: 482/124, 826/341, 648/432.

17. D. In each horizontal line there are four black circles and eight white. In each vertical line there are three black circles and six white.

18. Wish, yearn.

19. Attach, chance, cereal, allure, repeat.

20. 32814. Divide each number into three components and three sequences appear:

2, 4, 8, 16, 32
4, 5, 6, 7, 8
6, 8, 10, 12, 14

21. Corpuscle.

22. Ephemeral, evanescent.

23. E: Only lines that appear in the same position in the first two pentagons are carried forward to the third pentagon.

24. Disentangle.

25. Round table.

26. 9. Working along the diagonal lines, reverse and cancel out the lowest digit to make the next diagonal line: 387912 becomes 29783, etc.

27. Net; to get sonnet and network.

28. A. The pentagon turns around two sides clockwise.

29. Fit says = satisfy. The T words are typical (city pal), theater (hat tree), and tantrum (Mr. Taunt).

30. E. 1 is added to 2 to equal 3, etc.; 4 is added to 5 to equal 6, etc.; however, identically placed symbols disappear.

31. A. Dull red.

32. I. Start at the second letter C and work to alternate segments clockwise to spell out the word CIRCUIT.

33. Brainstorm.

34. Trout:

```
C  U  T  T  L  E
      B  R  E  A  M
      L  O  A  C  H
      T  U  N  N  Y
S  K  A  T  E
```

35. E. Looking both across and down, the contents of the third square are determined by merging the contents of the first two squares; however, when the same part of a curve appears in the same position in the first two squares, it is cancelled out in the third square.

36. Grosbeak.

37. Jubilant, exultant.

38. 83: 15 + 19 + 4 = 38, then reverse.

39. Trampoline.

40. A = 25. This is a square number; the rest are square numbers plus 1: $5^2=25$; $6^2-1=35$; $7^2-1=48$; $8^2-1=63$; and $9^2-1=80$

Test Three Questions

1.

7	4	8
3	2	6
9	5	3

is to

7	5	2
3	1	4
6	2	8

as

9	4	7
6	3	2
5	9	8

is to

?	?	6
?	?	?
?	5	?

2. Which is the odd one out?

mohair, chiffon, cashmere, angora, tweed

3. 74823 : 84327

and 27196 : 17692

therefore 52418 : ?

4.

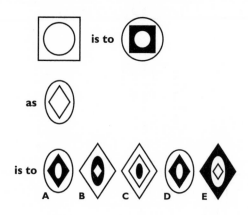

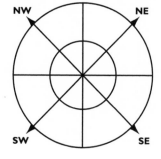

5. In a game of eight players that lasts for 70 minutes, two reserves substitute for each player so that all players, including reserves, are on the field of play for the same length of time. For how long is each player on the field of play?

6. Insert the letters into each quadrant so that two related 8-letter words can be read, one counterclockwise in the outer circle, and one clockwise in the inner circle.

NW : ACUR

NE : HIRD

SE : SEEN

SW : ACEE

7. 127, 168, 256, 300, ?

What number completes the above sequence?

8.

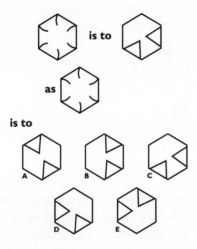

9. RAJ DOOLEY is an anagram of what two words that are opposite in meaning?

10.

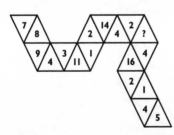

What number should replace the question mark?

11.

What comes next?

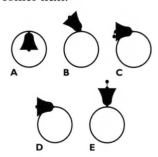

12. Find an 11-letter word or name by tracing from letter to connected letter. Letters are traced across the circle by chords; however, if the next letter is four letters or less away in the alphabet from the previous letter, it will be found by tracing around the circumference.

Clue: hobby for a peeping Tom? (7, 4 letters)

13. Only one set of five letters below can be arranged to spell a 5-letter English word. What is the word?

FAECY

ABTOP

MURCA

VENLO

IBEAL

14. What date comes 21 days after June 19?

15.

Which circle should replace the question mark?

16. fast : presto

  softly : a. piano
           b. largo
           c. lento
           d. andante
           e. legato

17. Below are six synonyms of the word GLOWING. Take one letter from each of the six synonyms in turn to find another synonym of GLOWING.

   suffused, luminous, aglow, warm, vivid, ruddy

18. What number should replace the question mark?

2	4
1	3
3	9

4	1
?	2
6	4

1	7
5	9
2	5

19. How many circles appear below?

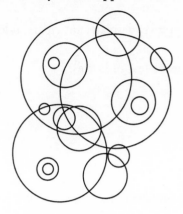

20. HEARS NO FUN is an anagram of what well-known phrase (3, 2, 8 letters)?

Clue: happy beam.

21. Which word in brackets is most opposite in meaning to the word in capitals?

PARAMOUNT (subordinate, proneness, scrupulous, predominate, inclination, peerless)

22. Place two 3-letter bits together to produce a type of boat.

CAR SAM WHA KER KEM LER TAN PAC PAM VER

23. Which two words are closest in meaning?

      fealty, diffident, approve, desolate, anticipate, fidelity

24. Which word below means fear of horses?

      cherophobia
      pantophobia
      selaphobia
      hippophobia

25. The average of three numbers is 16.
The average of two of these same numbers is 10.
What is the value of the third of the numbers if it is
two times the second number?

26. Use each of the 12 letters only once to spell out the
names of two types of dog.

    A D E O I K L L O S U P

27. Extract three digits from the list below which, taken in
the same order they appear in the list, are a third of the
number formed by the remaining digits.

    1   4   3   7   5   7   9

28. Complete the circles to find two words that are antonyms. The words may appear clockwise or counterclockwise.

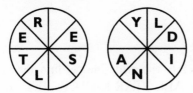

29. Which is the odd one out?

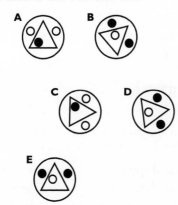

30.

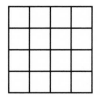

Put four 4-letter words into the grid, one per line, by using the letters of the phrase ALL STAR KARATE JET only once each. The four words, when placed correctly in the grid, will form a magic word square, where all four words appear both horizontally and vertically.

31. All of the vowels have been omitted from this trite saying. Can you work out the saying?

NJBSTSMLL TBTCH

32. CHASES LOVE is an anagram of what 2-word phrase?

33. Start at a corner letter and spiral round the perimeter clockwise to spell out a 9-letter word, finishing at the center square. You must provide the missing letters.

S   *   R

I   T   E

M   *   A

34.

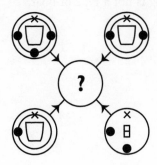

Each line and symbol that appears in the four outer circles above is transferred to the center circle according to these rules:

If a line or symbol occurs in the outer circles:
    once :   it is transferred
    twice: it is possibly transferred
    3 times: it is transferred
    4 times: it is not transferred

Which circle should appear in the center?

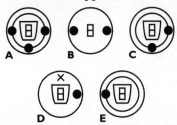

35. Which of the following is not a type of boat?

basseto
trireme
bireme
galiot
trimaran

36. What phrase is suggested below?

SELF

37.

Which circle below is most like the circle above?

38. 9495216859276834

What is the difference between the average of the sum of the odd numbers and the average of the sum of the even numbers?

39. Find an 8-letter word that when placed on the bottom line will complete eight 3-letter words reading downwards.

C	T	A	P	T	E	S	M
A	O	L	I	O	R	O	E
*	*	*	*	*	*	*	*

40. Insert the letters of the phrase RUINED FOOLS into the blanks to find two words that are opposite in meaning.

M******   M*****

Test Three Answers

1.   6   1   7

    3   2   8

    8   5   4

Rotate the first square 90º counterclockwise and reduce each number by 1.

2. Chiffon. It is silk, the rest are wool.

3. 42815. The position of the numbers change ABCDE to CBEDA.

4. B. The original figure goes inside the same shape that is originally on the inside. The middle portion is then shaded black.

5. 56 minutes: $\dfrac{70 \times 8}{10} = \dfrac{560}{10}$

6. Audience research.

7. 0. $(12 \times 7) \times 2 = 168$; $(16 \times 8) \times 2 = 256$; $(25 \times 6) \times 2 = 300$; $(30 \times 0) \times 2 = 0$.

8. E. Only the pairs of lines that curve toward each other in the first hexagon are converted to triangles in the second hexagon.

9. Ordeal, joy.

10. 6. Every straight line of numbers totals 28.

11. C. The bell moves 90° counterclockwise at each stage. The circle hangs naturally from the bell at each stage; therefore at the third stage it is inside the bell.

12. Lattice work.

13. Venlo = novel.

14. July 10.

15. B. Looking across and down the little hand moves 45° clockwise. Looking across, the big hand moves 90° clockwise, and looking down it moves 90° counterclockwise.

16. Piano.

17. Florid.

18. 7. The numbers formed by the top, middle, and bottom rows in the left and right rectangles total the numbers in the top, middle, and bottom rows in the middle rectangle: 24 + 17 = 41, 13 + 59 = 72, and 39 + 25 = 64.

19. 16.

20. Ray of sunshine.

21. Subordinate.

22. Whaler.

23. Fealty, fidelity.

24. Hippophobia.

25. 28. 6, 14, 28.

26. Saluki, poodle.

27. 459 x 3 = 1377

28. Secretly, candidly.

29. D. A is the same as C, and B is the same as E.

30.

S	A	L	T
A	J	A	R
L	A	T	E
T	R	E	K

31. No job is too small to botch.

32. Close shave.

33. Miscreant.

34. C.

35. Basseto (which is a musical term).

36. Alter ego.

37. D. It contains three white dots, two black dots, and a diamond.

38. 1. Odd: 9+9+5+1+5+9+7+3 = 48. 48/8 = 6.
        Even: 4+2+6+8+2+6+8+4 = 40. 40/8 = 5.

39. Tolerant.

40. Mindful, morose.

Test Four Questions

1. Which is the odd one out?

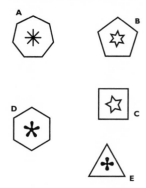

2. What is the longest word that can be spelled out by moving from letter to adjacent letter horizontally, vertically, and adjacently and not repeating a letter?

O	F	H	M	S
K	J	**I**	B	D
C	V	W	X	**R**
P	**L**	E	U	A
Y	G	T	N	Q

Clue: in a spirited manner

The three letters in bold appear in the word.

3. What number should replace the question mark?

4.

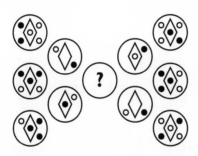

What should replace the question mark?

5. Decipher the code shown below on the telephone face below. Each number represents one of the letters shown with it on the telephone dial. A number does not represent the same letter each time.

	ABC	DEF
1	2	3
GHI	JKL	MNO
4	5	6
PRS	TUV	WXY
7	8	9
*	0	#

Dial a famous literary character: 48255323779 3466

6. SOLD DIREST ELK is an anagram of what familiar phrase (7, 2, 4 letters)?

Clue: fatal attraction.

7. What number should replace the question mark?

7	3	5	2
2	3	4	4
4	6	2	5
3	2	?	3

8.

What should replace the question mark?

A ○ B ◐ C ⊖ D ◉ E ●

9. Below are six antonyms of the word RIGID. Take one letter from each of the six, in order, and find another antonym of RIGID.

supple, elastic, yielding, lax, lenient, soft

10. Insert the letters to spell out two related words.

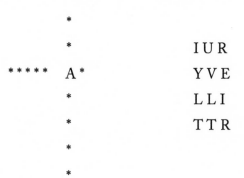

```
          *
          *              I U R
* * * * *  A *           Y V E
          *              L L I
          *              T T R
          *
          *
```

11. What number should replace the question mark?

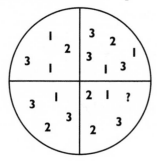

12.

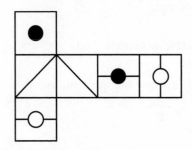

When the above is folded to form a cube, which is the only one of the following that can be produced?

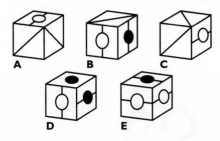

13. Which of the following is not an anagram of an animal?

coal pet

tent area

loan dog

fab foul

hen trap

14. Which is the odd one out?

drone, drawl, warble, articulate, prate

15. What number should replace the question mark?

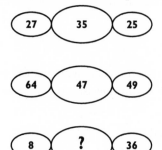

16.

What comes next?

17.

S	A	I		I	V	E
B	N	R		E	T	N
U	T	T	R	O	R	S
	I	P	U			

Move from letter to adjacent letter, horizontally, vertically, and diagonally, to spell out a 22-letter phrase. You must find the starting point and every letter must be used only once.

18. stalk: pedical

        petals : a. corolla
                  b. anther
                  c. pistil
                  d. nectary
                  e. stigma

19.

Find the starting point and work from letter to connected letter to spell out a 13-letter word. You can move any number of letters along a line, but stay on the lines only.

20. 45

72 54

31 27 ?

19 91 72 27

64 46 19 91

What number should replace the question mark?

21. What is the meaning of GELID?

    a. fatty
    b. fast moving
    c. extremely cold
    d. squashy

22. What word in brackets is most opposite in meaning to the word in capitals?

    LAUDABLE (quiescent, inferior, replete, proficient, theoretical, blameworthy)

23. ACTED IMMORAL is an anagram of what 12-letter word?

24.

What comes next?

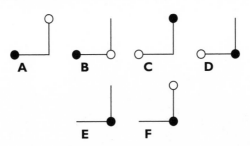

25. Place two 3-letter bits together to produce a 6-letter word that is a type of mineral.

SUM GRA MAR BEL COL PEW NIC GYP NIT TRE

26. Which three of the four pieces below can be fitted together to form a perfect square?

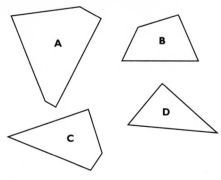

27. What number should replace the question mark?

1	9	4	7	6
2	8	3	8	4
1	3	6	7	8
4	9	2	9	8
2	3	4	?	2

28. What do all of these words have in common?

     shambles
     shareholder
     flamboyant
     purloined
     copied
     tribunal

29. Insert a 3-letter word that finishes the first word and starts the second.

     CAN   ***   ICE

30. Find a part of a sea-going vessel (5, 6 letters) by tracing from letter to connected letter. Letters are traced across the circle by chords; however, if the next letter is four letters or less away in the alphabet from the previous letter, it will be found by tracing around the circumference.

31. Which two words are closest in meaning?

reinstate, rectitude, rumination, concern, ascribe, integrity

32. Find the starting point and work clockwise to spell out a phrase (3, 2, 5, 5 letters). Only alternate letters of the phrase are shown.

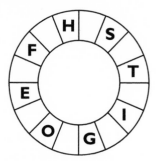

33. Place two 3-letter bits together to produce a word meaning a group of nine.

BEH ENN PEN AVE ALL OCT SPR UYE EAD TAD

34. Which is the odd one out?

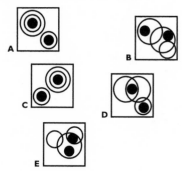

35. Alan has three times as many as Jane; however, if Alan and Jane give five each to Mary, who originally has none, Alan will then have five times as many as Jane and Mary will have twice as many as Jane. How many will each then have?

36. Which pair of letters is the odd one out?

LO   KP   GT   JQ   HS   FV

37. Complete the circles and find two words that are synonyms. The words might appear clockwise or counter clockwise.

38. Fill in the blanks to find a type of bird.

* * * * A B U * * *

39. Which of the following is not a geographical term?

    morass
    runlet
    bight
    defile
    anubis

40.

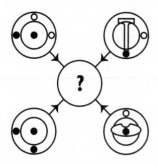

Each line and symbol that appears in the four outer circles above is transferred to the center circle according to these rules:

If a line or symbol occurs in the outer circles:

> once :   it is transferred
> twice: it is possibly transferred
> 3 times: it is transferred
> 4 times: it is not transferred

Which circle should appear in the center?

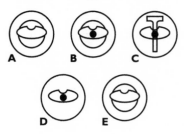

Test Four Answers

1. D. The number of arms on the star are one less than the number of side in the figure that contains it. In all the others the number of arms on the star is one more than the figure in which it is contained.

2. Vibrantly.

3. 2. The total of the numbers in each ring, starting with the inner ring (the bull's-eye), increases by 5 each time: 5, 10, 15, 20.

4. D. The contents of each circle are determined by the contents of the two circles immediately preceding it, working from each side toward the center. Only contents common to both these circles are carried forward to the next circle.

5. Huckleberry Finn.

6. Dressed to kill.

7. 5. So that each block of four numbers totals 15.

8. D. Divide the circles into groups, starting with the five circles at the extreme left. Each group is then repeated with the omission of the circle next to the extreme left (i.e. the second circle is omitted each time).

9. Pliant.

10. Virtual reality.

11. 3. Working counterclockwise from the upper left segment, the sum of the numbers in each segment increases by 2: 7, 9, 11, 13.

12. E.

13. Loan dog = gondola. The animals are: polecat (coal pet), anteater (tent area), buffalo (fab foul), and panther (hen trap).

14. Warble. It is a way of singing, the rest are types of speech.

15. 26. Cube root of 8 = 2, square root of 36 = 6.

16. A. A smaller circle is added each time and the ring next to the inside ring is shaded black.

17. It never rains but it pours.

18. Corolla.

19. Extraordinary.

20. 45. In each column take out the second smallest number from the previous column and reverse the digits in all the remaining numbers.

21. C. Extremely cold.

22. Blameworthy.

23. Melodramatic.

24. D. The black dot moves up and down and the white dot travels round the three points clockwise.

25. Gypsum.

26.

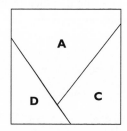

27. 9. 23 x 4 = 92. The same rule applies in all other lines: 19 x 4 = 76; 28 x 3 = 84; 13 x 6 = 78; 49 x 2 = 98.

28. They all contain food s(ham)bles, s(hare)holder, f(lamb)oyant, pur(loin)erd, co(pie)d, tri(bun)al.

29. Not.

30. Ship's anchor.

31. Rectitude, integrity.

32. One of those things.

33. Ennead.

34. B. All the others contain one dot that's in two circles and one dot that's in one circle.

35. Alan 25, Jane 5, Mary 10.

36. FV. The remaining letters are the same distance from the beginning and end of the alphabet respectively.

37. Inactive, sluggish.

38. Kookaburra.

39. Anubis (a jackal-headed god in Egyptian mythology).

40. C.

Test Five Questions

1.

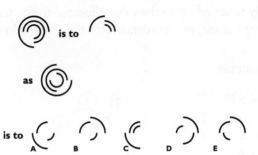

2. viable : feasible

      realistic : a. plausible
              b. definite
              c. valid
              d. uncertain
              e. conceivable

3. What do these words have in common?

    soothsay
    spongiform
    payable
    Hamlet
    drift
    smuggler
    plenipotent

4. Insert the remaining numbers 1 to 6 into the circles, using each number once, in such a way that for any particular circle the sum of the numbers in the circles connected directly to it add up to the value allocated to the number inside the circle, in accordance with the chart below.

Example:

4 = 5 (3 + 2)
3 = 6 (4 + 2)
2 = 8 (4 + 4 + 1)
1 = 2

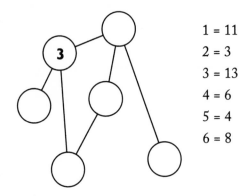

1 = 11
2 = 3
3 = 13
4 = 6
5 = 4
6 = 8

5.

What comes next?

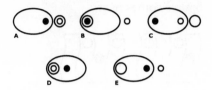

6. Attracting or compelling notice or attention.
Which word below is closest in meaning to the definition above?

    a. exquisite
    b. important
    c. tangible
    d. prominent
    e. supreme

7. Which is the odd one out?

    adobe, wigwam, pavilion, big top

8. What number is 35 less than when multiplied by 6 times itself?

9.

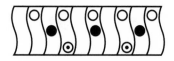

Which block of four figures comes next?

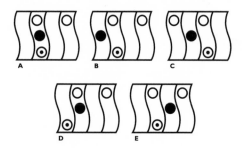

10. Find the starting point, and by following the directions visit every square once only, to finally arrive at the square with the treasure (marked T).

    1S
    2W
    means 1 square South and 2 squares West.

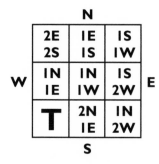

11. Complete the words so that the same two letters that finish the first word start the second word, and the same two letters that finish the second word start the third word, etc. The same two letters that finish the fourth word also start the first word, to complete the circle.

     * * A N * *

     * * E N * *

     * * L I * *

     * * I T * *

12. What number should replace the question mark?

13. Which is the odd one out?

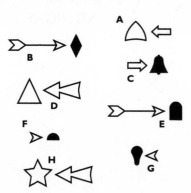

14.

T S M O	E E U C	N S I S
A O N N	R N T I	F N A B
F S I W	O T C O	E A A A

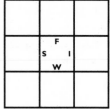

Rearrange the remaining eight blocks around the center one so that each two adjacent letters spell out a 2-letter word (12 in total), and the name of a U.S. city can be read clockwise around the outer perimeter.

15. Insert the letters into each quadrant so that two related 8-letter words can be read, one counterclockwise in the outer circle and one clockwise in the inner circle.

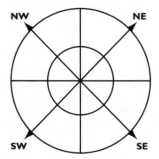

NW : TLUA
NE : RONE
SE : ROCS
SW : PEMP

16. What number should replace the question mark?

3	7	2	6
4	1	5	8
6	4	5	3
5	6	?	1

17.

What is missing?

18.   SUNDAY
MONDAY
TUESDAY
WEDNESDAY
THURSDAY
FRIDAY
SATURDAY

What day comes two days before the day that comes immediately after the day that comes three days before the day immediately before Saturday?

19. What is the longest English word that can be produced from the following ten letters?

HUEBOLPNEC

20. What number should replace the question mark?

1858 : 3629
2742 : 5421
1994 :   ?

21. What is a fritillary?

a. a butterfly
b. lace work
c. wind chimes
d. a group of ships

22. What number should replace the question mark?

68352 : 57461
32768 : 41857
27436 :   ?

23. Which two words are closest in meaning?

pernicious, enduring, legitimate, prosaic, objection, baneful

24. Which word in brackets is most opposite in meaning to the word in capitals?

CONTENTIOUS (concerned, obedient, stubborn, unswerving, puerile)

25. Complete the circles to find two words that are antonyms. The words may appear clockwise or counterclockwise.

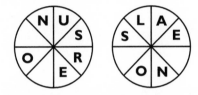

26. Which is the odd one out?

27.

Which number is the odd one out?

28. Try to solve the following, each of which represents an English word. For example: xqqqqqq = excuse (xqs).

nnnnick
.ically

29.

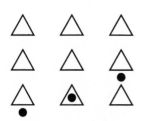

What comes next?

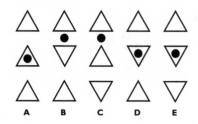

30. Which five of the six pieces below can be fitted together to form a perfect square?

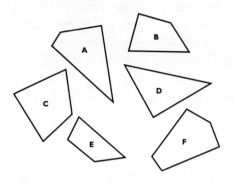

31. Which word in column B belongs in column A?

A	B
comedy	lie
bird	wash
treacle	elephant
widow	mark
	heat

32. The ages of five family members total 114 between them.

Alan and Sue total 50 between them.
Sue and Sheila total 42 between them.
Sheila and Mike total 54 between them.
Mike and David total 33 between them.

How old is each family member?

33. LOCAL DRAINS is an anagram of what type of geographical feature?

34. Find a 14-letter word by moving from letter to adjacent letter in any direction, including diagonally. Two letters are not used, and all other letters can be used only once.

S	O	E	I
C	C	R	R
N	N	P	E
E	D	O	S

35. In how many of the following will a knot be formed when both ends of the string are pulled simultaneously?

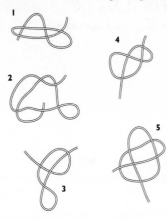

36. A 2-word phrase where each word starts with the same letter has had its initial letters removed and has been made into one word. For example, TOP TEN would appear as OPEN. What phrase has been so disguised below?

ETAIL

37. What number should replace the question mark?

17	4	6	78
19	9	8	80
16	7	9	81
15	7	8	64
14	2	6	?

38. Decode the following short phrase (5, 4 letters) in which each letter has been substituted for its corresponding number in the alphabet (A =1, B = 2, C = 3, etc.). For example, the word CODE would appear as 31545: C(3), O (15), D (4), E (5).

51712552554

39. Find an 8-letter word to place on the bottom line that will complete eight 3-letter words reading downwards.

S	S	T	C	O	P	A	U
A	K	O	U	F	E	R	S
*	*	*	*	*	*	*	*

40.

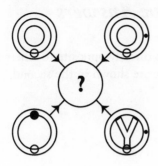

Each line and symbol that appears in the four outer circles above is transferred to the center circle according to these rules:

If a line or symbol occurs in the outer circles:

> once : it is transferred
> twice: it is possibly transferred
> 3 times: it is transferred
> 4 times: it is not transferred

Which circle should appear in the center?

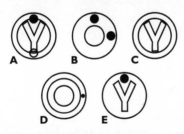

Test Five Answers

1. A. Only the parts of arcs directly opposite to where a gap appears in the first figure are shown in the second.

2. Conceivable.

3. They all contain trees in reverse:

    soot(hsa)y - ash
    spon(gif)orm - fig
    pa(yab)le - bay
    Ha(mle)t – elm
    d(rif)t – fir
    s(mug)gler – gum
    pl(enip)otent – pine

4.

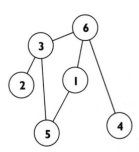

5. E. The small white dot is moving left to right, the large circle moves from side to side inside the ellipse, and the black dot moves in and out of the ellipse on the right-hand side.

6. D. Prominent.

7. Adobe; it is a building material whereas all the others are types of tent.

8. 7.

9. A. Every second figure contains a white circle at the top, every third figure contains a black circle in the center, and every fourth figure contains a white circle with a dot at the bottom.

10.

4	7	2
6	3	8
T	I	5

11. Orange, genial, allied, editor.

12. 7 : 73^2 = 5329, similarly 39^2 = 1521 etc.

13. G. In all the others, arrows point left to white figures and right to black figures.

14.

```
  F     R     A
N  A  N  T  O  N
  B     I     N
  E     F     O
A  A  S  I  T  C
  A     W     O
  T     E     N
S  M  E  U  S  I
  O     C     S
```

San Francisco appears clockwise around the outer perimeter.

15. Personal computer.

16. 6. Each horizontal and vertical line of four numbers totals 18.

17. D. To complete every combination in sets of three of the three different figures: circle, square, triangle.

18. Monday.

19. Opulence.

20. 3847: 19 x 2 = 38, 94 / 2 = 47

21. A. A butterfly.

22. 18345. Add 1 to the odd digits and deduct 1 from the even digits.

23. Pernicious, baneful.

24. Obedient.

25. Uncovers, conceals.

26. E. It contains an extra white star.

27. 49. It is a square number, the rest all being square numbers reversed.

28. Forensic, periodically. (Score 1 point for one correct and a bonus point for both correct!)

29. D. The dot moves up in its position at each stage, and when it appears in a triangle, that triangle is inverted.

30.

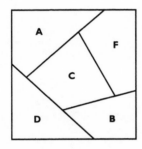

31. Mark. All words in column A can be prefixed with black, and all words in column B can be prefixed with white.

32. Alan 47, Sue 3, Sheila 39, Mike 15, David 18.

33. Coral island.

34. Correspondence.

35. Numbers 3 and 4 will form a knot.

36. Set sail.

37. 72: (14-2) x 6.

38. Eagle-eyed.

39. Typeface.

40. E.

Test Six Questions

1.

Which is the missing segment?

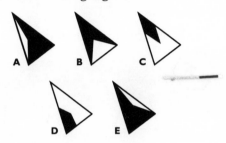

2. genuine : bona fide

actual: a. de facto
b. a priori
c. compos mentis
d. fait accompli
e. pari passu

3. Work from letter to adjacent letter horizontally, vertically, and diagonally to spell out a 12-letter word. You must provide the missing letters. Every letter is used only once.

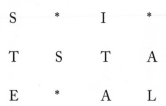

S	*	I	*
T	S	T	A
E	*	A	L

4. What number should replace the question mark?

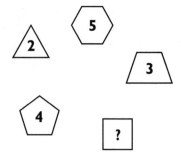

5.

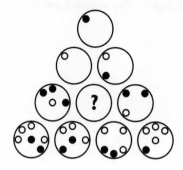

What circle should replace the question mark?

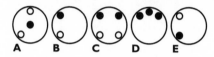

6. Which word in brackets is closest in meaning to the word in capitals?

SEDITIOUS (mutinous, immune, alluring, motionless, cryptic)

7. Insert a word in brackets that will form a new word when tacked onto the end of DAY and a different word when placed before PIECE.

DAY (   ) PIECE

8. What number should replace the question mark?

```
                        8

                7               8

        8               5               ?

    7               5               8               3

3               8               5               2               7
```

9.

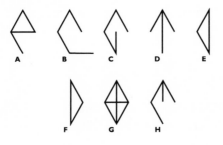

What comes next?

10. To make holy by religious rule or word.
What word below is most opposite in meaning to the definition above?

    a. destroy
    b. profane
    c. hallow
    d. disdain
    e. sequester

11. Insert a word in the parentheses that means the same as the definitions outside the parentheses.

    cram or wedge (   ) fruit preserve

12. How many minutes is it after 10 a.m. if 30 minutes later it will be half as many minutes before 12 noon?

13. Which is the odd one out?

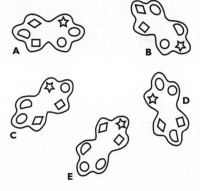

14.   A   B   C   D   E   F   G   H

What letter is two to the right of the letter that is five to the left of the letter immediately to the right of the letter two to the left of the letter H ?

15. The following is an anagram for a well-known phrase. The number of letters in each word of the phrase is indicated in the parentheses.

heigh-ho! To warmer cell (4, 4, 2, 4, 5 letters)

16. What number should replace the question mark?

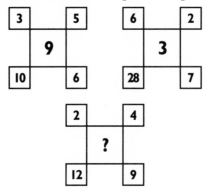

17.

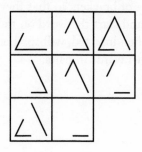

Which is the missing tile?

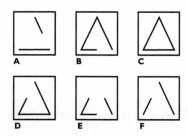

18. Which word in brackets is most opposite in meaning to the word in capitals?

ARID (fresh, soft, lax, fetid, humid)

19. Insert two letters in each set of brackets so that they finish the word on the left and start the word on the right. The correct letters, when inserted, will spell out an 8-letter word when read downwards in pairs.

SE (* *) E N

T H (* *) V Y

S L (* *) L E

B A (* *) S S

20. What number should replace the question mark?

35	81	?
64	72	58
29	96	43

21. Which word in brackets means the same as the word in capitals?

ESCULENT (edible, rancid, cumbersome, prevailing, offensive, association)

22. What phrase is suggested below?

23. Which two words are most opposite in meaning?

genial, animated, eminent, torpid, vindictive

24. Which two shapes are identical?

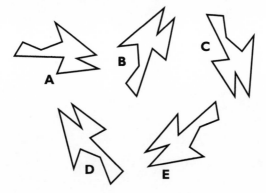

25. What are always part of an entrechat?

     a. teeth
     b. ears
     c. eyes
     d. legs
     e. a ski slope

26. Change one letter only in each word below to produce a familiar phrase.

    if no car at

27. What number should replace the question mark?

	3	
1	3	9
0	1	5
6	8	?
1	3	9

28. Find a 9-letter word by moving from letter to adjacent letter in any direction including vertically. Each letter must be used only once and you must provide the missing letter.

O	Z	I
O	W	N
*	S	E

29. My watch needs a new battery. Although it was correct at 1 p.m., it then began to lose 15 minutes each hour. It now shows 5:15 p.m., but it stopped six hours ago. What is the correct time now?

30.

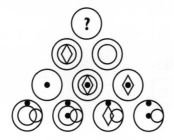

Which circle should replace the question mark?

31. What number should replace the question mark?

		4		3		
5			5		6	
		?			6	
						4
	8		8			
						5
	5					

32. Place two 3-letter bits together to produce a type of color.

NGI YEL DIN COP LET VIO GOL ORA LOI RER

33. What number should replace the question mark?

26	6	14	142
19	7	17	116
21	9	26	163
18	5	20	?

34. What kind of creature is a lamprey?

    a. bird
    b. fish
    c. mammal
    d. insect

35. All the vowels have been removed from the following saying, and the remaining letters split into groups of four. Replace the vowels and rebuild the quote.

FLSR SHNW HRNG LSFR TTRD

36.

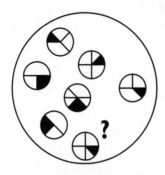

Which circle should replace the question mark?

37. What is the next number in this series?

67, 80, 88, 104, 109, 119, ?

38. Complete the circles to find two words that are similar in meaning. The words may appear clockwise or counter clockwise.

39.

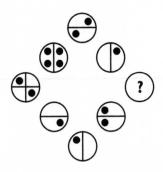

Which circle below should replace the one with the question mark?

40. Which is the odd one out?

       run-of-the-mill
       eye shadow
       all-or-nothing
       foreign office
       minor key
       don't know

Test Six Answers

1. E. Opposite segments have black/white reversal.

2. A. De facto.

3. Systematical.

4. 3. Each number is one less than the number of sides in the figure in which it is contained.

5. B. The contents of each circle are determined by the dots which are common to these two circles are carried forward; however, they then change from black to white and vice versa.

6. Mutinous.

7. Time.

8. 7. Start at the bottom and reverse the previous row, dropping the lowest number each time.

9. C. Working clockwise, each line of the diamond is perpendicular in turn.

10. B. Profane.

11. Jam.

12. 60 minutes.

13. E. Shapes are in the same order clockwise inside the cloud in A and D, and in B and C.

14. D.

15. Come hell or high water.

16. 6. 2 x 9 = 18, 12 / 4 = 3, 18 / 3 = 6.

17. D. Looking both across and down, the contents of the third square are determined by the contents of the first two. Only lines that are common to these first two squares are not carried forward to the third square.

18. Humid.

19. Amenable.

20. 17. Start at the bottom left-hand square and work up the first column, then back down the second, then up the third repeating the digits 296435817 in the same order.

21. Edible.

22. Learning curve.

23. Torpid, animated.

24. B and C.

25. D. Legs (it is a leap in ballet).

26. In so far as.

27. 4. 1061 x 3 = 3183 x 3 = 9549.

28. Wooziness.

29. 1 a.m.

30. E. Each pair of circles produces the circle above by carrying forward only those elements that are different. Similar elements are cancelled out.

31. 7. Each number represents the number of blank squares immediately surrounding it in the grid.

32. Violet.

33. 70. (18 x 5) − 20 = 70.

34. B. Fish.

35. Fools rush in where angels fear to tread.

36. C. Each circle will then have a mirror of itself.

37. 130. Each number is obtained by adding to the previous number the digits that make it up: 67 + 6 + 7 = 80; 80 + 8 + 0 = 88, etc.

38. Abundant, generous.

39. E. Look along rows of three circles in any direction. You will find that the contents of the third circle in each row is determined by merging the contents of the previous two circles, except that like symbols disappear.

40. Eye shadow. It contains YES embedded in it (e(ye s)adow). The remaining phrases have NO embedded in them.

Test Seven Questions

1. Work from letter to adjacent letter horizontally, vertically, and diagonally to spell out a 12-letter word. You must provide the missing letters; every letter is used only once.

I	*	G	N
T	L	E	A
S	I	E	*

2. What number should replace the question mark?

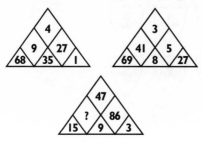

3. Move from circle to circle to spell out a 10-letter word, avoiding wrong turns and using every letter only once.

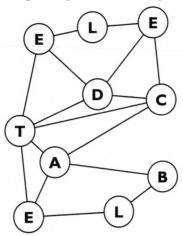

4.

Which is the missing shield?

5. What letter should replace the question mark?

A	C	F
E	G	J
J	?	O

6. What phrase is suggested by the arrangement of letters below?

FFEARW

7. What number should replace the question mark?

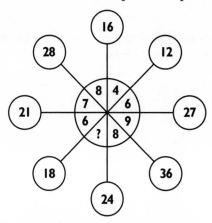

8.

What comes next?

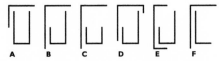

A   B   C   D   E   F

9. Add one letter, not necessarily the same letter, to the beginning, middle, or end of each word to produce two new words that are similar in meaning.

    ROW SELL

10. Insert an historical event into the end column to complete the 3-letter words reading across.

T	A	*
D	U	*
H	I	*
L	I	*
T	O	*
F	A	*
H	A	*
S	E	*
T	E	*
M	A	*
P	E	*
S	I	*
N	O	*
L	A	*

11. What number should replace the question mark?

24	39	41	71	51
?				32
67				29
64				81
45	25	55	57	72

12. How many triangles appear in this figure?

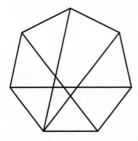

13. Complete the words. One reads clockwise and the other counterclockwise (you must figure out which). The words are similar in meaning. You must provide the missing letters.

14. Arrange the letters in the squares to find two 9-letter words, one in each square, that are synonyms.

O	I	I	
T	E	N	U	U
V	A	L	D	L
	E	I	S

(grid as shown)

O	I	I
T	E	N
V	A	L

and

U	U
D	L
E	I	S

15. How many minutes is it after 12 noon if 52 minutes ago it was five times as many minutes past 10 a.m.?

16.

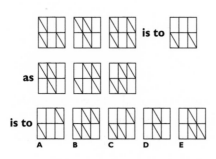

17. Change one letter only in each word below to produce a familiar phrase.

SIT FOE RAT

18. harass : harry

       sortie : a. charlie
                b. sally
                c. hector
                d. victor
                e. patsy

19. What number should replace the question mark?

	9	5	
5	6	3	8
7	4	5	?
	7	9	

20.

To which box below can a dot be added so that both dots then meet the same conditions as in the box above?

  A   B   C   D   E

21.

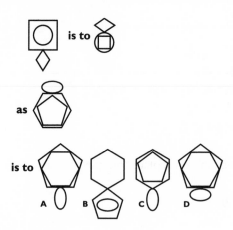

22. I TEST SEWER is an anagram of what phrase (5, 4 letters)?

23.   2753 : 7246

6492 : 3507

5861 :   ?

24. Which two words are most opposite in meaning?

remorse, artifice, worry, honesty, suspicion, change

25. Which of the following is not an anagram of a nautical term?

on guard
go amber
big red
chain me
drew ale

26. What phrase is suggested below?

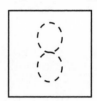

27. What number should replace the question mark?

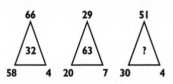

28. Which is the odd one out?

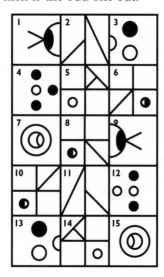

29. Find a 10-letter word by moving from letter to letter and using every letter only once.

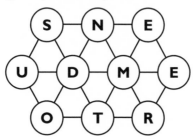

30. Each of the nine squares in the grid marked 1A to 3C should incorporate all the lines and symbols shown in the squares of the same letter and number immediately above and to the left. For example, 2B should incorporate all the lines and symbols that are in 2 and B.

One of the squares is incorrect. Which one is it?

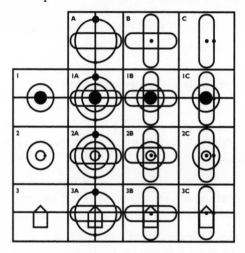

31.

? 9h2 0

Draw the figure that should replace the question mark.

32. What letter is missing?

33. Use all of the letters of the following words once only to spell out the names of four U.S. cities.

Elegant, tenable, civil, servant, doodle

34. The following is an anagram of a well-known phrase. The number of letters of each word in the phrase is indicated in parentheses.

The woody generator room (4, 5, 4, 8 letters)

35. Complete the circles and find two words that are antonyms. The words may appear clockwise or counter clockwise

36. Find a 9-letter word by moving from letter to letter in any direction, including vertically. You may use each letter only once.

I	E	A
D	W	W
E	K	A

37. Find an 9-letter word to insert on the bottom line to complete eight 3-letter words reading downwards.

H	C	P	E	P	P	I	T
A	O	A	M	I	A	C	O
*	*	*	*	*	*	*	*

38.   2
12
1112
3112
211213
312213
212223
114213
31121314
41122314
31221324
?
?

What are the next two numbers in this sequence?

39. Add three consecutive letters of the alphabet to the group of letters below to form a 6-letter word.

ATE

40. How many lines appear below?

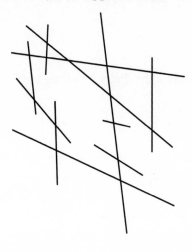

Test Seven Answers

1. Evangelistic.

2. 2. Each triangle contains the digits 1 to 9 each only once.

3. Delectable.

4. B. Each line and each column of shields contains one inverted figure and one figure shaded black.

5. L. Looking across, the sequence runs: skip one letter, then two: AbCdeF. Looking down, skip three letters, then four: AbcdEfghiJ.

6. Few and far between.

7. 6. 6 x 6 / 2 = 18; similarly, 6 x 7 /2 = 21, 7 x 8 / 2 = 28, 8 x 4 / 2 = 16, etc.

8. B. At each stage, half a side of the large rectangle disappears and half a side of the small rectangle is added.

9. Grow, swell.

10. Boston Tea Party.

11. 15. Opposite numbers as shown in the diagram below, total 96.

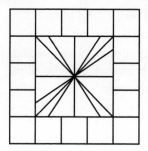

12. 14.

13. Frenzied, maniacal.

14. Inviolate, unsullied.

15. 17 minutes.

16. C. Only vertical lines that appear in the same position twice in the first three squares are carried forward to the final square.

17. Tit for tat.

18. Sally.

19. 8. Multiply the numbers found on the outside to obtain the numbers formed in the middle opposite: 5 x 7 = 35, 9 x 5 = 45, 8 x 8 = 64, 7 x 9 = 63.

20. D. One dot appears in an apex created by one curved and one straight line, and the other dot appears in a section created by two straight and one curved lines.

21. A. The pentagon and hexagon trade places so that the hexagon is now inside the pentagon, and the ellipse rotates 90° and goes to the bottom.

22. Street wise.

23. 4183. Both numbers in each analogy total 9999: 5861 + 4138 = 9999.

24. Artifice and honesty.

25. Chain me = machine. The nautical terms are: aground (on guard), embargo (go amber), bridge (big red), leeward (drew ale).

26. Pieces of eight.

27. 84. (51 − 30) x 4.

28. 10. The rest are in mirror image pairings: 1/9, 2/11, 3/13, 4/12, 5/24, 6/8, 7/15.

29. Tremendous.

30. 2C.

31.

Turn the page upside down to see why. They are the even numbers 0, 2, 4, 6, 8 in reverse order and upside down.

32. X. Do that the letters when rearranged spell HEXAGON, the figure in which they are contained.

33. Cleveland, Galveston, Detroit, and Abilene.

34. Here today gone tomorrow.

35. Separate, coalesce.

36. Wideawake.

37. Splutter.

38.   21322314
        21322314
Each number describes the number above, starting with the lowest digits first.
So, 3112 contains 2 1s, 1 2s, 1 3s and thus the number on the next line is 211213.
21322314 recurs, and the sequence is ended.

39. A**stu**te.

40. 11.

Test Eight Questions

1.

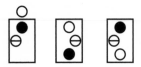

What comes next?

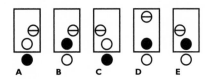

2. Move from letter to adjacent letter, horizontally, vertically, and diagonally to spell out a 22-letter phrase. You must find the starting point and every letter must be used only once.

I	H	N		O	F	A
N	I	C		T	R	L
A	A	N	O	E	T	L
	E	T	H			

3. A   Z   C   W   E   T   G   ?

Which letter comes next in the above sequence?

4. What number should replace the question mark?

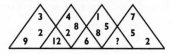

5.

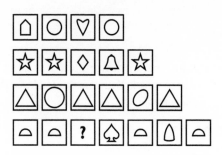

What should replace the question mark?

6. Add one letter, not necessarily the same letter, to the beginning, middle, or end of each word to produce two new words that are opposite in meaning.

SICK   RUDE

7. Add one letter, not necessarily the same letter, to each word (beginning, middle, or end), to find seven words that all have something in common.

RUB   FAN   INK   CAN   BACK   OLD   CRAM

8. Find the starting point and work from letter to connected letter to find a 13-letter word. You can move along the line. One letter is used twice.

9. 1.5, 3.25, 5, 6.75, ?

What number continues the above sequence?

10.

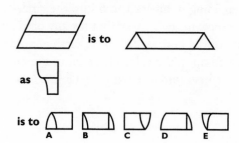

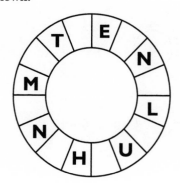

11. Find the starting point and find a familiar phrase (2, 8, 6 letters) reading clockwise. Only alternate letters are shown.

12. Which is the odd one out?

estuary, peninsula, gulf, lagoon, sound

13. Insert the remaining numbers 1 to 6 into the circles, using each number once, in such a way that for any particular circle the sum of the numbers in the circles connected directly to it add up to the value allocated to the number inside the circle in accordance with the table below.

Example:

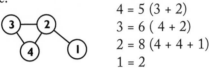

4 = 5 (3 + 2)
3 = 6 (4 + 2)
2 = 8 (4 + 4 + 1)
1 = 2

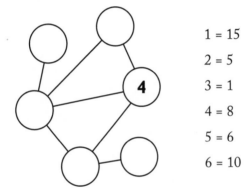

1 = 15

2 = 5

3 = 1

4 = 8

5 = 6

6 = 10

14. Which is the odd one out?

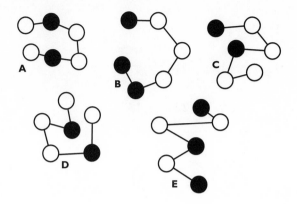

15. Complete the words, one reads clockwise and the other counterclockwise (you must figure out which). The words are opposite in meaning. You must provide the missing letters.

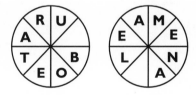

16. Insert a word in parentheses that means the same as the definitions outside the parentheses.

cast off (   ) small building

17. What number should replace the question mark?

1	2	3	5
92	149	214	8
?	35	22	13

18.

What comes next?

19. pioneer : innovate

trigger : a. embark
b. launch
c. develop
d. actuate
e. institute

20. 10, 10, 8.5, 11.5, 7, 13, ?

What number comes next?

21. Which word in brackets is similar in meaning to the word in capitals?

PROFLIGATE (exuberance, laconic, auger, debauched, restrained, obtruce)

22. Place the nine 3-letter bits together to produce three 9-letter words.

HIN   TLE   DIS   IST   SOR

SUC   MAC   CES   MAN

23. Which is the odd one out?

A

B

C

D

E

F

24.

Arrange the digits 1-9 in the circles in such a way that:

> Numbers 1 and 2 and all the digits between them add up to 10.
> Numbers 2 and 3 and all the digits between them add up to 45.*
> Numbers 3 and 4 and all the digits between them add up to 29.
> Numbers 4 and 5 and all the digits between them add up to 17.

Hint: * Make this your starting point.

25. What is always part of FRUCTOSE?

> a. sugar
> b. salt
> c. coffee beans
> d. rice
> e. cake

26. barrel, prison, plural, cleric, ?

What word below continues the sequence above?

famous, shroud, glutton, chaotic, prism

27. Find the value of X in the equation below:

$$(3^2)(8^2) = X3^3$$

28. Complete the circles and find two words that are synonyms. The words may appear clockwise or counterclockwise.

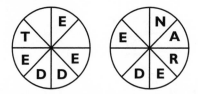

29. Find a 10-letter word by moving from letter to letter. Each letter must be used only once.

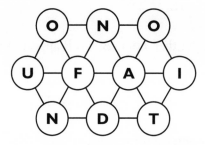

30. Find the name of a sea creature (7, 5 letters) by tracing from letter to connected letter. Letters are traced across the circle by chords, however, if the next letter is four letters or less away in the alphabet from the previous letter, it will be found by tracing around the circumference.

Clue: Can this creature find the sunshine?

31. In how many different ways can you arrange the letters in the word ARRANGE?

Hint: You must consider that letters A and R appear in the word twice.

32. Change nine to six with just one stroke of the pen.

33. Decode the following short message.

TMUEEESTDMAEY

34. Find a 14-letter word by moving from letter to adjacent letter in any direction (including vertically). Two letters are not used and the remaining letters can be used only once.

N	I	T	C
A	R	N	O
B	T	I	D
I	L	O	N

35.   timelessly
        levitation
        tastefully
        effrontery

What word comes next in the above sequence?

    rockabilly, oncologist, receptacle, obediently, economical

36. What is the collective noun for a group of spiders?

    a. cluster
    b. leash
    c. rayful
    d. rout
    e. nest

37. Which anagram is not a type of food?

ligcar
cussid
genaro

38.

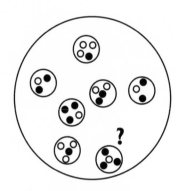

Which circle should replace the question mark?

A   B   C   D   E

39. Find the number that comes next in this sequence.

355
410
425
440
?

40.

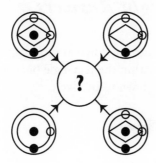

Each line and symbol that appears in the four outer circles above is transferred to the center circle according to these rules:

If a line or symbol occurs in the outer circles:

        once: it is transferred
        twice: it is possibly transferred
        3 times: it is transferred
        4 times: it is not transferred

Which circle should appear in the center?

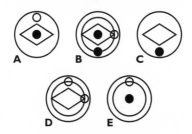

Test Eight Answers

1. B. The white circle is moving down at each stage and the other two circles stay within the rectangle but move from side to side across and down respectively

2. Not for all the tea in China.

3. Q. There are two alternate sequences moving forward and back in the alphabet respectively: AbCdEfG and ZyxWvuTsrQ.

4. 9. The numbers at the bottom are the sums of numbers that appear only once in adjoining sections: 12 = 9 + 3 and 4 + 8 (because 2 is common to both sections and, therefore, not used). Similarly 6 = 4 + 2 and 1 + 5 (8 is common); and 9 = 8 + 1 and 7 + 2 (5 is common).

5. D. The first line has two symbols alike, the second line three symbols alike, the third line four symbols alike; therefore, the fourth line has five symbols alike.

6. Slick, crude.

7. All colors: ruby, fawn, pink, cyan, black, gold, cream.

8. Atmospherical.

9. 8.5. Add 1.75 each time.

10. A. The top half is folded onto the bottom half.

11. No laughing matter.

12. Peninsula. Peninsula is land; the rest are sea.

13.

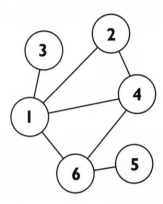

14. C. A is the same chain as D and B is the same as E.

15. Obdurate, amenable. The missing letters are d and b.

16. Shed.

17. 57. Start at the top left and work along the top row, down the last column, back along the bottom, then up and along the middle row, adding each two numbers to arrive at the third number: 1 + 2 = 3, 2 + 3 = 5, 3 + 5 = 8, etc. So: 22 + 35 = 57.

18. B. The large outer arc moves 180° at each stage, the middle arc moves 90° clockwise, and the inner arc moves 90° counterclockwise.

19. Actuate.

20. 5.5. There are two alternate sequences, subtracting 1.5 and adding 1.5 respectively

21. Debauched.

22. Machinist, dismantle, successor.

23. E. All the others are divided into four equal segments.

24. 2 7 1 6 4 8 5 9 3 or 3 9 5 8 4 6 1 7 2

25. A. Sugar.

26. Shroud. The vowels *aeiou* are being repeated in the same order.

27.   64. (3^2) (8^2) = X9
       $9 \times 64 = 9X$
          $64 = X$

28. Demented, deranged.

29. Foundation.

30. Basking shark.

31. 10080 ways:

$$\frac{8 \times 7 \times 6 \times 5 \times 4 \times 3 \times 2 \times 1}{2 \times 2} \text{ (because the letters A and R appear twice)}$$

32. IX + S = SIX

33.

M	E	E	T	M	E	
T	U	E	S	D	A	Y

34. Indoctrination.

35. Oncologist. Each word begins with the middle two letters of the preceding word.

36. A. Cluster.

37. Cussid = discus. The foods are ligcar = garlic, genaro = orange.

38. B. Each circle in the large circle pairs with another containing the same number of black dots and white dots.

39. 455. The numbers are clock times, without the colon, with 15 minutes added each time: 3:55, 4:10, 4:25, 4:40, 4:55.

40. A.

Test Nine Questions

1.

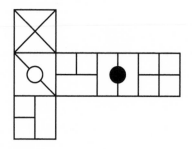

When the above is folded to form a cube, which is the only one of the following that can be produced?

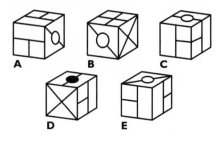

2. WHAT GREAT KISS is an anagram of what two words that are opposite in meaning?

3. Change one letter of each word below to produce a familiar phrase. (Hint: The phrase has already appeared in this book.)

OLD ORE CUT

4. How many minutes is it before 12 noon if 16 minutes ago it was three times as many minutes past 9 a.m.?

5.

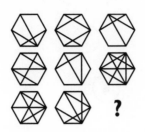

Which hexagon is missing?

6. smooth : mellifluous

rough : a. abrasive
b. rasping
c. brusque
d. jagged
e. curt

7. Which is the odd one out?

puzzle, predicament, poser, enigma, conundrum

8.

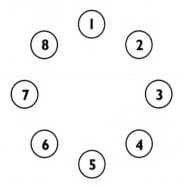

What circle is directly opposite the circle that is three places clockwise away from the circle that is one place counterclockwise away from the circle that is directly opposite the circle one place counterclockwise from circle number 4?

9. Only one set of five letters below can be rearranged to spell a 5-letter English word. What is the word?

NELOW
RALTO
DOINT
TOBAL
HUCAL
GECPO

10.

Which shield below has most in common with the shield above?

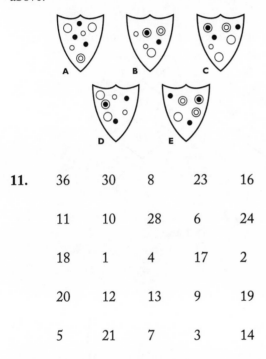

11.

36	30	8	23	16
11	10	28	6	24
18	1	4	17	2
20	12	13	9	19
5	21	7	3	14

What number is two places away from itself doubled, three places away from itself halved, one place away from itself plus 2, three places away from itself less 1, three places away from itself plus 5, and two places away from itself plus 3?

Diagonal places are included.

12. Which of the following is not an anagram of a type of food?

assuage
am Lisa
Paul sat
dung dip

13. What number should replace the question mark?

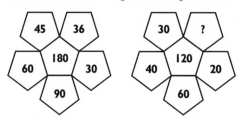

14.

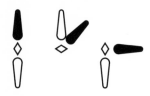

What comes next?

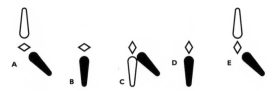

15.

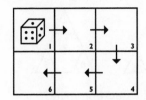

A die is rolled one face to square 2, and so on, one place at a time to squares 3, 4, 5, 6 in turn. What number will appear on the top face in square 6?

16. The following clue leads to what pair of rhyming words?

impressively large group of musicians

17.   562 : 17

483 : 28

792 : ?

18.

*	R	E	A		
U	L	U	F		
A	D	E	O	*	N
R	E	T	S	I	V
	G	I	E	O	
	A	T	*	N	

Find the starting point and work from letter to letter horizontally, vertically, or diagonally to find a well-known institution. All letters are used only once, and you must provide the three missing letters.

19.

What number should replace the question mark?

20. Which four of the six pieces can be fitted together to form a perfect square?

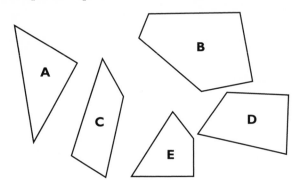

21. Which word in brackets is similar in meaning to the word in capitals?

INVETERATE (machination, frankness, preamble, confounded, established, creative)

22. Place two 4-letter bits together to produce an 8-letter word that is a type of boat.

BILA AREN SCHO FIRE COAL SHOP
BOOT TRIM ONER NDIR

23. Insert the letters of the phrase LOVE TORN RIVALS into the gaps to form a palindromic phrase, i.e., one such as Madam I'm Adam, which reads the same backwards and forwards.

*A*S *I** *N ** E*** *T**

24.

2	7	2	9		3	8	2	6
1	3	8	4		4	9	7	8
4	1	1	3		8	?	?	4

What numbers should replace the question marks?

25. Find a 14-letter word by moving from letter to adjacent letter in any direction, including vertically. Two letters are not used, and the remaining letters can be used only once.

L	O	G	N
E	E	R	I
N	I	O	U
A	T	N	M

26. Which is the odd one out?

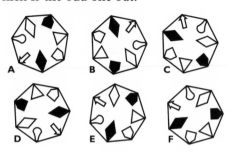

27. Can you identify the names contained within the following phrases?

sound as a bell
apple sauce
raise the roof
hurricane lamp
whoopee cushion

28. What number should replace the question mark?

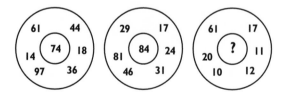

29. beverage
elevator
vendetta
dominate

What comes next?

abdicate, invasion, identity, mackerel, intercom

30. Find the name of a Jurassic flying reptile (11 letters) by tracing from letter to connected letter. Letters are traced across the circle by chords; however, if the next letter is four letters or less away in the alphabet from the previous letter, it will be found by tracing around the circumference.

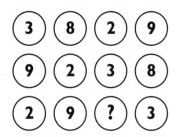

What number should replace the question mark?

32. Which two words are most opposite in meaning?

specific, modicum, aggregate, rapacious, abundance, raucous

33. Change one letter only in each of the following words to produce a familiar phrase.

BUT NO SET

34. 16, 21, 19.5, 18.25, 23, 15.5, ?

What two numbers come next?

35. Complete the circles to find two words that are antonyms. The words may appear either clockwise or counterclockwise.

36. Which two words are the odd ones out?

sordid

age	not	cat
toiled	ear	odd
tangle	octant	old

unbolt   pedlar

37. 29, 18, 47, 28, 75, ? , ?

Which two numbers come next?

38. Insert the name of a major U.S. city in the third column reading downwards in order to complete ten 3-letter words reading across.

P	A	*
H	U	*
H	O	*
T	O	*
T	A	*
P	A	*
C	U	*
S	E	*
M	A	*
H	A	*

39. Find a 10-letter word by moving from letter to letter using each letter once each only

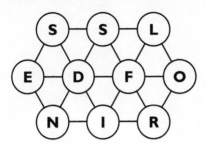

40.

Which circle should replace the question mark?

Test Nine Answers

1. A.

2. Askew, straight.

3. Odd one out.

4. 41 minutes.

5. B. Looking across and down, only lines that appear once in the first two hexagons are carried forward to the third hexagon. Lines that appear twice in the same position are cancelled out.

6. Rasping.

7. Predicament. It is a condition of difficulty; the rest are hard-to-solve problems.

8. 5.

9. Tobal = bloat.

10. D. It contains three black dots, two white dots, and three large circles.

11. 6.

12. Spatula = Paul sat. The foods are sausage (assuage), salami (am Lisa), pudding (dung dip).

13. 24. The numbers around the outside can all be divided evenly into the number in the center.

14. A. The white arm moves 180° at each stage and the black arm moves 45° clockwise at each stage. The diamond moves 90° at each stage.

15. 4.

16. Grand band.

17. 25: 9 x 2 + 7

18. Federal Bureau of Investigation. Missing letters: FBI.

19. 3: 7 + 8 = 15 / 5 = 3

20.

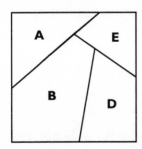

21. Established.

22. Schooner.

23. Rats live on no evil star.

24. 8 and 0. 3826 + 4978 = 8804 (2729 + 1384 = 4113)

25. Mountaineering.

26. F. The rest contain the same sequence of figures. F has two of these figures reversed.

27. They have all Biblical characters embedded in them:

> sound as (a bel)l
> appl(e sau)ce
> rai(se th)e roof
> hurrican(e lam)p
> whoopee (cush)ion

28. 51. Left-hand numbers minus right-hand numbers: 61 + 20 + 10 − 17 − 11 − 12

29. Invasion. Each word begins and ends with the middle two letters of the previous word.

30. Pterodactyl.

31. 8. Each horizontal line contains the same four numbers. Each column contains three out of the four of these same numbers.

32. Modicum, abundance.

33. Put to sea.

34. 26.5, 12.75. There are two alternate series; +3.5 and -2.75

35. Cowardly, fearless.

36. Ear and pedlar. Pedlar contains the letters ear in the sequence *E**AR. The remaining pairings are in the sequence *A*G*E, as in age and tangle. The remaining pairings are not/unbolt, odd/sordid, old/toiled, cat/octant.

37. 35, 100: 2 x 9 = 18, 29 + 18 = 47; 4 x 7 = 28, 47 + 28 = 75; 7 x 5 = 35, 75 + 35 = 110

38. New Orleans.

39. Floridness.

40. E: x + y = z and r + s = t. However, similar symbols disappear.

Test Ten Questions

1. Which is the odd one out?

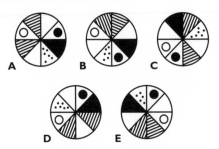

2. Which two words are most opposite in meaning?

demand, impede, negate, ignore, provide, assert

3. What do all the following have in common?

pate de fois gras
jalapeno pepper
gas turbines
Notting Hill
Baker Street
magnetic declination

4. During the morning I visit three stores. After visiting the first store, I am left with just 40% of the original sum of money I set out with; at the second store I spend one third of the remainder. I then visit the third store with my new balance and spend 0.2 of it, which leaves me with a final amount of $12. How much money did I start out with?

5. lavish : sumptuous

august : rarefied
         month
         venerable
         pretentious

6.

Which hexagon should replace the question mark?

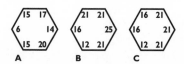

7.

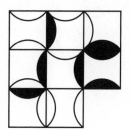

Which is the missing tile?

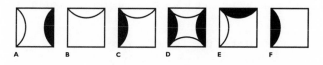

8. Which two words are closest in meaning?

expand, espouse, efface, embrace, escort, evade

9.   13249 : 127

51672 : 138

28614 : ?

10. Which is the odd one out?

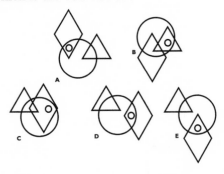

11. What phrase is suggested below?

*ND   PARC**

12. The following clue leads to what pair of rhyming words?

tore text of play

13.

What comes next?

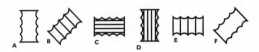

14. The following clues are solved by what two words, both starting with the same four letters, which are reversed in the second word. For example, **car**toons and **trac**tion: cart and trac.

  characterization in a play or film
  very hot and humid

15. Which two words that sound alike, but are spelled differently, mean:

  brandish, renounce

16. What number should replace the question mark?

	7
10	8
14	12
19	17
25	14
32	?

17.

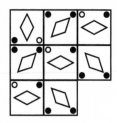

Which is the missing tile?

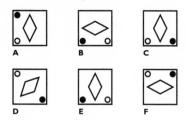

18. RENAME PIE BOX is an anagram of what two words that are similar in meaning?

19. 4628 : 545

3917 : 654

7531 : ?

20. Spiral clockwise to find a 10-letter word. You must find the starting point and provide the missing letters. The word you are looking for starts and finishes with the same two letters.

21. Which two words are most opposite in meaning?

cordial, exculpate, remoteness, proximity, imposing, propitious

22. Which word in brackets is similar in meaning to the word in capitals?

INEXORABLE (immature, inestimable, infallible, incapable, inscrutable, implacable)

23. How many minutes is it before 6 p.m. if 20 minutes ago it was three times as many minutes past 4 p.m.?

24.

Which is the missing tile?

25. What number should replace the question mark?

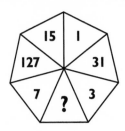

26. Change one letter only in each of the following words to produce a familiar phrase.

MAP SO CAN

27. What number should replace the question mark?

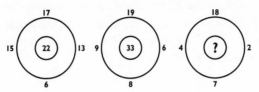

28.

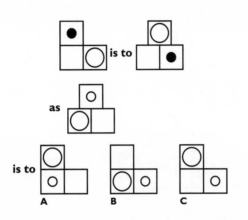

29. Find a trite saying, known as Ornstein's Law, in which all the vowels have been removed, and the consonants arranged into five groups. In each group the letters are in the correct order; however, the groups are not in the correct order. (For example, FIND THE TRITE SAYING could appear TRTSY NG FNDTH.)

SGNTH CDG NBDYV TSYSN RPTST

30. Each of the nine squares in the grid marked 1A to 3C should incorporate all the lines and symbols shown in the squares of the same letter and number immediately above and to the left. For example, 2B should incorporate all the lines and symbols that are in 2 and B.

One of the squares is incorrect. Which one is it?

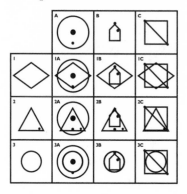

31. Which of the following is not an anagram of a country?

regalia
median
serial
enemy

32. What number should replace the question mark?

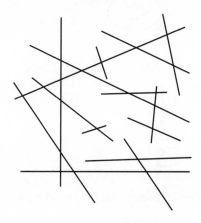

33. How many lines appear below?

34. What number should replace the question mark?

35. Which is the odd one out?

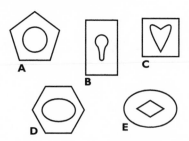

36. What number should replace the question mark?

9		4		1
8	2	9	3	?
4		2		4

37. Change one letter only in each word to produce a well-known phrase.

HIM ON MOSS

38.

What comes next?

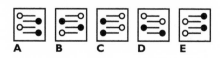

39. Find a 10-letter word by moving from letter to letter, using each letter only once.

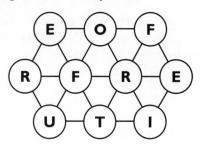

40. Which is the odd one out?

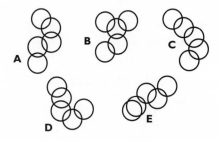

Test Ten Answers

1. C. In all the others, horizontal stripes are opposite spots, vertical stripes are opposite the black dot, and black is opposite the white dot.

2. Negate, assert.

3. They all contain three consecutive letters of the alphabet.

> pate (de f)ois gras
> jalape(no p)epper
> ga(s tu)rbines
> Nottin(g Hi)ll
> Bake(r St)reet
> magneti(c de)clination

4. $56.25. Working back: $12 + 25% = $15 + 50% = $22.50 / 0.4 = $56.25

5. Venerable.

6. B. To obtain the number in each apex, add the number in that same apex in the previous hexagon to the number next to it, working clockwise: 10 + 11 = 21, 11 + 14 = 25, etc.

7. C. Take arcs forward to the third square, both across and down, only when they appear in the same position just only in the first two squares; however, these arcs change from white to black and vice versa in the third square.

8. Espouse, embrace.

9. 129. 2 + 6 + 4 = 12, 8 + 1 = 9

10. B. In all the others the dot appears in the circle and diamond.

11. Part and parcel.

12. Ripped script.

13. E. The figure tumbles over 45° each time and alternates horizontal stripe, vertical stripe, blank.

14. Portrayal, tropical.

15. Wave, waive.

16. 12. Start at 7 and work down the left side adding 3, 4, 5, 6, 7. The numbers down the left side are 7 plus the sum of digits on the left side, i.e. 7 + 1 + 0 = 8, 7 + 1 + 4 = 12. Therefore, 7 + 3 + 2 = 12.

17. E. There are three combinations of dots; each row and column contains one of the combinations. Also working across and down, the diamond is rotating 45° at each stage.

18. Probe, examine.

19. 642. The second numbers are the average of each pair of numbers in the four-figure number: 7 and 5 = average 6; 5 and 3 = average 4; 3 and 1 = average 2.

20. Originator.

21. Remoteness, proximity.

22. Implacable.

23. 25 minutes.

24. D. Each row and column includes one each of the three types of star and one of the stars is shaded black.

25. 63. Start at 1 and jump to alternate segments clockwise, doubling each number plus 1 each time: 1 + 1 + 1 = 3, 3 + 3 + 1 = 7, etc.

26. Man to man.

27. 22. (17 – 6) x (15 – 13); (19 – 8) x (9 – 6); (19 – 7) x (4 – 2)

28. B. The block at the top trades places with the block bottom right.

29. Nobody ever puts out a sign that says nice dog.

30. 2B.

31. Median = maiden. The countries are Algeria (regalia), Israel (serial), Yemen (enemy).

32. 30. 9 − 4 x 6

33. 15.

34. 14. It's the difference between the number formed on the left and right sides: 29 and 15.

35. E. It is a straight sided figure in a curve-sided figure. The rest are all curve-sided figures within straight-sided figures.

36. 6: 984 / 2 = 492; 492/3 = 164

37. Hit or miss.

38. C. A new line is added at the top each time, alternating right facing/left facing and with white/black dots.

39. Forfeiture.

40. B. All the others are a continuous single chain.